That's Science?

Bad Hair Days
and Other Experiments

Kirsten Weir

SCHOLASTIC INC.

New York   Toronto   London   Auckland   Sydney
Mexico City   New Delhi   Hong Kong   Buenos Aire

Illustrations
Tom Nick Cocotos

Developed by ONO Books in cooperation with Scholastic Inc.

Text copyright © 2003 by Scholastic Inc.
Illustrations copyright © 2003 by Tom Nick Cocotos.
All rights reserved. Published by Scholastic Inc.
Printed in the U.S.A.

ISBN 0-439-59788-9

1 2 3 4 5 6 7 8 9 10   08   12 11 10 09 08 07 06 05 04 03

Contents

Welcome to This Book

Do bad hair days wreck your mood? Wonder why? Do you remember sports stats but forget important dates in history? Wonder why? Ever wonder where belly-button lint comes from? Well, wonder no more.

Believe it or not, these questions have scientific answers. You just have to know how to look for them. And the scientists in this book have looked for answers in some pretty strange places.

So start reading. You'll be saying, "That's science!" in no time.

Target Words These words will help you find answers to some very, um, *interesting* questions.

- **data:** facts or information
  Scientists collect and study data.

- **observation:** the careful watching of someone or something
  Observation is how scientists learn about the world around us.

- **study:** a test to see if an idea is right
  Scientists conduct studies to gather information.

Reader Tips Here's how to get the most out of this book.

- **Follow Procedures** Science is a step-by-step process. Scientists follow a specific procedure when conducting experiments. This is known as the scientific method. If one step is missed, the results will not be correct. Check out the steps of the scientific method on page 7.

- **Summarize** A summary is a short report about the most important ideas. As you read, summarize the most important points. That way you will be sure to understand what you've read.

1

Science at Work

How do scientists figure it all out?

What is science, anyway? Well, there are two basic kinds. Some scientists study nature. They look at how plants grow. They study the way the heart works. They use a telescope to study the stars. This kind of science is called natural science.

Other scientists study people. They ask what makes us happy or sad. They study what we buy and why. They look at how we relate to other people. This kind of science is called social science.

Scientists study different things. But they all follow strict rules when they work. They ask their questions in the same way. And they look for answers in the same way. The rules they follow are called the **scientific method.**

The Scientific Method

1. Make **observations.**

Let's say your little brother is sick. You notice that he gets sick a lot. That's an observation. But why is he sick so much?

2. Take a guess. State your **hypothesis.**

What do you think is going on? Maybe your brother only gets sick when he has a test.

3. Just do it. Set up your **experiment.**

That's a test to find out facts. And it takes time to do it right. So, take a whole school year. Count the number of times your brother stays home sick. Count how many times he's sick on a test day. Keep good notes. You'll need them for the next step.

4. Get results. Add up the **data.**

What information did you gather? How many sick days? How many test days? How many were both? Do the math.

5. Find meaning in the data.

State your **conclusion,** or what you found. Is your brother mostly sick on test days? If he is, your hypothesis was right. Your brother isn't really sick. He's sick of tests!

Your Nose Knows

Do scents add up to dollars?

Does the smell of French fries make you hungry? Does the stink of a locker room gross you out?

Smells can affect how we feel. But can smells control how we act? Alan Hirsch wanted to find out. He's a brain scientist. So he used the scientific method to put sniffers to the test.

OBSERVATION: Hirsch studies how smells affect the brain. For example, the scent of lavender can make you feel calm. That's because lavender wakes up a certain part of the brain. It's the part that tells your body to relax.

This made Hirsch wonder. Smells can change how we feel. But can they change what we do?

HYPOTHESIS: Hirsch took his question to the mall. Malls are full of smells like food, perfume, and leather. Could those smells make us want to shop till we drop? Hirsch guessed that scents can make people want to spend money.

EXPERIMENT: Hirsch bought two pairs of sneakers. They were exactly the same. Then he found two rooms. They were exactly the same.

Next, he put one pair of sneakers in each room. But he sprayed one room with a flower scent. That was the scented room. He left the other room without any scent. That was the unscented room.

Hirsch had 35 people take turns going into each room. They looked at both pairs of sneakers. Then they answered a list of questions. They told which sneakers they liked best. They also said how much they'd pay for each pair.

Heads Up!

The two rooms and the two pairs of shoes are exactly the same. Why is that important?

DATA: Hirsch studied the data from the **surveys.** What did he find? Eight out of ten people liked the shoes in the scented room best. And they said they would pay about $10 more for that pair.

CONCLUSION: Hirsch proved his hypothesis. The scent of flowers made people **prefer** the shoes in one room even though they were *exactly* the same as the shoes in the other room. It also made them willing to pay more for them!

Hirsch says that stores do lots of things to get you in the mood to spend. They control the lights. They choose the colors. They make sure the store is the right temperature. They play music. And they use scents, too.

So next time you open your wallet, stop for a minute. Ask yourself, Do I really need that? Or am I just being led by my nose?

Heads Up!

Does this experiment change how you feel about shopping now? Why or why not?

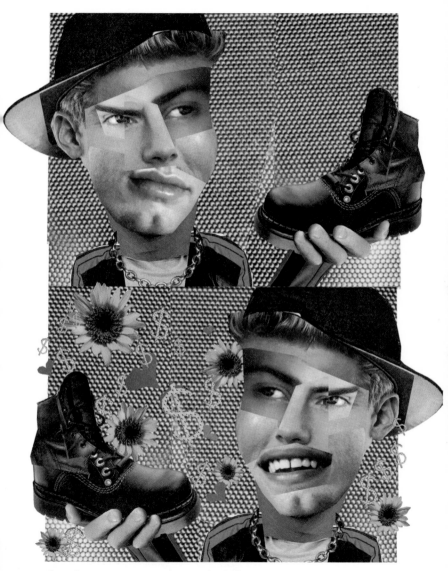

Certain scents can make you feel like a big spender.

Under Control

Why did Alan Hirsch use two rooms in his **study**? After all, he only cared if people would like the shoes in the scented room.

But suppose he used only one room. And suppose he found out that his **subjects** liked the shoes a lot. What would that prove? Maybe that they were really nice shoes.

Hirsch needed what scientists call a control. He needed to compare a scented room to an unscented room. So he made everything in both rooms the same. Everything, that is, except the thing he was trying to measure — how a scented room affects shoppers.

So one room had no smell at all. That was the control room. The other room smelled like flowers. That was the experimental room. And that's how he could see if scent made the difference.

Now that's good science.

Bad Hair Days

Can bad hair wreck your whole day?

Sometimes it's frizzy. Sometimes it's flat. Sometimes it sticks up in a weird way. It won't behave no matter what you do.

Everybody has bad hair days. But Marianne LaFrance felt there might be more to bad hair days than, well, bad hair. She wanted to check it out. Do bad hair days mess with moods? To find out, she fired up the scientific method.

OBSERVATION: LaFrance studies how people's looks make them feel. She once told a friend that her hair didn't look very good. Her friend turned grumpy. That made LaFrance wonder. How much do bad hair days affect our moods?

HYPOTHESIS: How does funky hair make you feel? LaFrance formed a hypothesis about that. She guessed that people would say they felt lousy on bad hair days. And she also thought bad hair would bug girls more than guys. Hmm. We'll see about that!

EXPERIMENT: To test her idea, LaFrance set up a study. She used 120 subjects. She split them into three groups. And she didn't tell the subjects what the experiment was about.

LaFrance asked Group 1 to remember a bad hair day.

Group 2 was the control group. She didn't ask them to think about anything.

LaFrance asked Group 3 to think about a time they had trouble opening a package. "We wanted people to think about a bad experience that had nothing to do with their **appearance**," LaFrance said. That way she could compare bad feelings about hair to other bad feelings.

Next she made the subjects take tests. The tests asked questions about their mood.

DATA: LaFrance collected the data from the tests. She sorted the tests by each group. She sorted the tests filled out by men and the ones filled out by women.

What did the data tell her? The people who remembered a bad hair day felt the worst of the three groups.

CONCLUSION: LaFrance was right. Bad hair can make your **self-esteem** suffer. But she wasn't right about everything.

She had guessed that women would feel worse than men. Sure, women felt unhappy about bad hair. But men felt just as bad. They felt less smart and less brave. And they didn't want to be around other people.

What did LaFrance learn? A bad hair day can get anyone down.

Heads Up!

How did LaFrance show the effects of bad hair on people? Why did she need three groups to show this?

A bad hair day is enough to put anyone in a bad mood.

More, More, More

LaFrance tested 120 people in her experiment. That seems like a lot of work. Wouldn't it be easier just to test three people? Sure. But it wouldn't be good science.

The number of subjects LaFrance had is called her **sample size.** The bigger a sample size is, the better. Why?

Testing one person tells you mainly about that person. Testing a lot of people helps you find an overall trend.

Say LaFrance studied three people. And suppose she learned that all were upset by a bad hair day. Maybe those three people were just very into their looks.

But what if she found out that a hundred people were bugged by bad hair? Then she might have found a general pattern.

There's one more thing. A sample should include many different kinds of people, too. Think about it. What if LaFrance tested 120 fashion models? Or 120 firefighters? Do you think the results might have been different?

Drill It Into Your Head

How do your feelings affect your memory?

·Do you remember what you wore last Sunday? How about what you ate for dinner two weeks ago? Not likely.

But what if it was your birthday two weeks ago? Would you remember that you had a pizza party? Would you remember that you wore your new shirt?

Or what if you watched a creepy movie that night? Would you remember tossing your popcorn high into the air? Would you remember that you forgot a sweater because you kept shivering from fear?

Psychologist Kristy Nielson wondered if strong **emotions** help your memory. So she went looking for a link between emotions and memory. And she used the scientific method, of course.

OBSERVATION: Nielson had noticed that people seemed to remember powerful events in detail. They seemed to remember less about boring events. (Hmmm. Is that why you always say, "Nothing," when people ask you what you did in school all day?)

Nielson had also learned from lab tests. Rats remembered the path through the maze when they were under **stress.**

Could stress do the same thing for humans? she wondered.

HYPOTHESIS: Nielson guessed that stress makes people's memories sharper. She thought stressed subjects would remember the event that stressed them. She guessed they would remember other boring details about the event, too.

―**Heads Up!**―
Look up stress *in the glossary. Think of a time when you were under stress. Do you have clear memories of what happened?*

A dentist's drill might sharpen your memories!

EXPERIMENT: Nielson found 32 subjects to help her. She asked them to read a list of words like "queen" and "butterfly." Then she split them into two groups.

Nielson's experiment was a **blind study.** None of the people knew what it was about. Nielson didn't want them acting differently than they normally would.

Nielson showed one group a dull video about brushing teeth. Yawn.

She showed the other group a different video. It showed a dentist drilling and pulling out a patient's teeth. "I find the idea of drilling your teeth to be really creepy," Nielson said. "It's not so fun to watch."

The day after showing the videos, Nielson tested all the subjects. She asked them to remember the words from the day before.

---**Heads Up!**-----------------

Which group do you think will remember more of the words? Why?

DATA: So, who remembered the most words? The people who watched the tooth-drilling video.

CONCLUSION: Nielson studied the results. And what was her conclusion? Exciting or stressful events improve memory. Stress helps people remember things.

Nielson thinks **adrenaline** helps lock memories in the brain. Adrenaline is a chemical that the body releases when it's under stress.

And there might be a good reason why this happens. Remembering a scary event can protect us from getting into danger in the future.

Nielson believes that any strong feelings can improve memory. Laughing your head off might work, too. Try it when you study for your next big test.

Keepin' It Real

Social scientists make great spies. They love to watch people. And they like it best when people have no idea they are being watched. That's because social scientists study human **behavior.** They want the behavior to be as natural as possible.

But social scientists can't just go around spying. They need to set up their experiments carefully. They use the scientific method. They use control groups. They need large samples.

So, how do scientists get their subjects to act naturally during an experiment? They run blind studies.

In a blind study, the subjects don't know the purpose of the study. Nielson's subjects didn't know why they watched a tooth-drilling video. And they didn't know that other people were watching a different video. That way they couldn't cheat—accidentally or on purpose.

Often scientists don't know which subjects are in which group. They only learn this after the data is collected. That's called a **double-blind study.** That way the scientists know they have treated the control group and the experimental group exactly the same way.

Fuzzy Navels

Why are some belly buttons filled with fluff?

Dr. Karl Kruszelnicki has a science radio show in Australia. One day a caller asked where belly-button lint comes from. Strangely enough, Dr. Karl didn't hang up on him. Dr. Karl lives for crazy questions like this one. So he set out to solve the mystery of fuzzy navels.

OBSERVATION: Dr. Karl doesn't get much belly-button lint. So he couldn't observe himself. Instead, he asked around to get information from other people.

Dr. Karl met a man named Doug. Doug had once shaved off the hair around his belly button. His navel stopped filling with lint. Then the hair grew back. The fuzz came back, too.

That gave Dr. Karl an idea.

HYPOTHESIS: Dr. Karl guessed that belly-button lint was mostly **fibers** from clothes. He also guessed that hairy bellies trapped the fibers. Then the hair pulled them into the belly button.

EXPERIMENT: Dr. Karl wrote a survey of 19 questions about belly-button lint. He asked the subjects if they were male or female. And he asked if they had hair on their bellies. He put the survey on the Internet. That way people all over the world could reply.

Dr. Karl asked people to send samples of their lint. He wanted to look at it under a **microscope.** Then he could see what was in it.

DATA: Almost five thousand people filled out Dr. Karl's survey. A few actually dug out some lint and sent it in.

Here's what Dr. Karl found. Seven out of every ten people had belly-button lint. Of those, almost three out of four were men.

Dr. Karl also found that belly-button lint is made of clothing fibers. And it's stuck together with bits of dead skin. Ewwww.

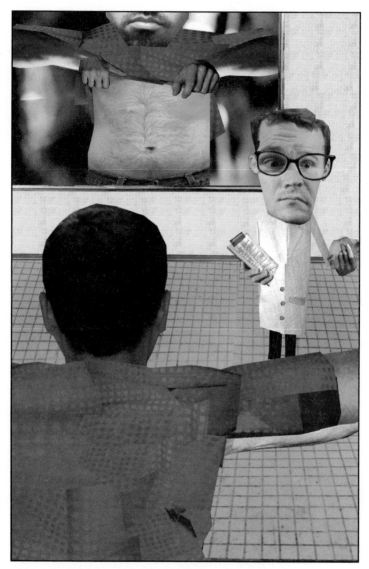

Now you know where belly-button lint comes from.

Conclusion: Dr. Karl learned that you're most likely to get belly-button lint if you have two things. One is a hairy belly. And the other is an innie. "Hair carries fluff into the big hole," he said.

But people who aren't hairy sometimes get lint, too. Dr. Karl has a possible explanation. He thinks these people wear tight shirts. He thinks tight clothes move fuzz into the navel the same way hair does.

Why did Dr. Karl take on the belly-button lint? Well, it was fun. Besides, he said, "You never know where science will take you."

Heads Up!

Dr. Karl thinks that tight clothes also cause belly-button lint. What kind of experiment could you do to find out if this is true?

Who Dreamed Up the Scientific Method?

In the old days, people answered questions just by thinking about them. If an answer made sense, that was good enough. But then René Descartes (day-KART) changed all that.

Descartes was born in France in 1596. He solved difficult math problems. And he wanted a way to prove that his answers were right. He slept on it. And the solution came to him in three strange dreams.

Here are the rules he dreamed up:

1) Don't assume anything. Believe only things that can be tested and proved.

2) Break big problems down into small parts. Solving the parts will help solve the big problem.

3) Start with simple things—things you can prove. Use them to prove more complex ideas.

4) Don't let your personal feelings get in the way of the facts.

And that was how Descartes dreamed up the scientific method.

René Descartes dreamed up the scientific method.

Kissing Right

Most people are right-handed. When it comes to kissing, are they also right-headed?

Onur Güntürkün (Gyoon-tyoor-kyoon) likes watching people kiss. No, he's not a creep. It's his job. And for the sake of science, Onur turned to the scientific method.

OBSERVATION: Most people are right-handed. Most people prefer to use their right foot, right eye, and right ear, as well. Onur knew all this. He studies why our brains choose a favorite side.

Onur had also noticed something else. Most unborn babies turn their heads to the right while still inside Mom. But what about adults? he wondered. Are most grownups "right-headed"? The answer could give him one more clue about how the brain works.

Do most people tilt their heads to the left or to the right?

HYPOTHESIS: Onur guessed that most adults are "right headed." But how would he test that? What makes people turn their heads?

Then it hit him. Why not study kissing couples? They have to tilt their heads to keep from bumping noses. He guessed that most people turn to the right before locking lips.

EXPERIMENT: To answer his question, Onur became a spy. He secretly watched couples kiss. But he wondered: What if people from different **cultures** kiss in different ways?

So, he tried to watch kissers from different countries. He watched lovebirds in Turkey, Germany, and the United States. And he hung out in international airports and bus stations to watch kissers from lots of cultures.

Onur set other rules, too:

1. Only the first kiss counts.
2. Only lip-to-lip kisses count.
3. Kissers can't be holding anything that gets in the way.
4. It has to be clear which way the kissers turn their heads.

Data: Onur spied on kissers for more than two years. When he finished, he had watched 124 kissing couples. Eighty turned their heads to the right. That's two out of three people.

Conclusion: Onur's hypothesis was right. Most people are "right-headed." His study was simple. It didn't cost much. But it gave Onur another clue about how our brains work. One day it might help him understand how people make plans and decisions.

Onur did have some surprises. "A few couples managed to kiss without tilting their heads!" he said. "They had little noses."

Heads Up!

Onur Güntürkün guessed that most adults were "right-headed." What observations led him to this guess?

Try It Yourself

Put the scientific method to the test on your next test!

OBSERVATION: Say you have to memorize the countries in Europe. You're finding it really hard. In English class you have to memorize a short poem. That's not so hard. Why?

HYPOTHESIS: The words in a poem all relate to each other. Related words are easier to remember. But a list of countries is just a list. Unrelated words are harder to remember.

EXPERIMENT: Get a bunch of friends together. Split them into two groups. Give one group this list of words: apple, doubt, lake, sneeze, cookie.

Give them one minute to learn all the words. Tell them they have to learn them in that order.

After one minute, give them each a paper and pen. Ask them to write down the list of words.

Then give the list to the second group. But this time, give them this sentence along with the list. *All dogs love Swiss cheese.* Explain that the words in the list begin with the same letters (*a*pple and *a*ll; *d*oubt and *d*ogs, etc.).

Give group two the same one-minute test.

DATA: Which group was able to remember more words?

CONCLUSION: Take a look at your hypothesis again. Was it right? If so, you might have a brand new studying weapon.

Use the scientific method to answer your own questions.

Want some more experiment ideas? Try these Web sites:

Cool Science for Curious Kids:
www.hhmi.org/coolscience/

The Science Club: Kids' Science Projects:
www.scienceclub.org/kidproj1.html

Try Science:
www.tryscience.org

Funology.com: The Laboratory:
www.funology.com/laboratory/index.cfm

Glossary

adrenaline *(noun)* a chemical in the brain (p. 22)

appearance *(noun)* the way someone or something looks (p. 14)

behavior *(noun)* the way people act (p. 23)

blind study *(noun)* a study in which none of the subjects know what it is about (p. 21)

conclusion *(noun)* the findings at the end of an experiment (p. 7)

culture *(noun)* the ideas and habits of a group of people (p. 32)

data *(noun)* facts or information (p. 7)

double-blind study *(noun)* a study in which neither the subjects nor the scientists know the makeup of the experiment (p. 23)

emotion *(noun)* feeling (p. 18)

experiment *(noun)* a test designed to prove something (p. 7)

fiber *(noun)* a thread or tiny piece of cloth (p. 25)

hypothesis *(noun)* a guess or idea that is tested in a science experiment (p. 7)

microscope *(noun)* a machine that lets you see tiny objects up close (p. 25)

observation *(noun)* the careful watching of someone or something (p. 7)

prefer *(verb)* to like one thing better than another (p. 10)

psychologist *(noun)* a person who studies minds and behavior (p. 18)

sample size *(noun)* the number of people or things tested in a scientific study (p. 17)

scientific method *(noun)* the step-by-step system by which scientists solve problems (p. 6)

self-esteem *(noun)* the way a person feels about himself or herself (p. 15)

stress *(noun)* worry, strain, or pressure (p. 19)

study *(noun)* a test to see if an idea is right (p. 12)

subject *(noun)* a person who takes part in an experiment (p. 12)

survey *(noun)* a list of questions used in an experiment (p. 10)

Index